THE
GREAT WALL
OF CHINA

THE
GREAT WALL
OF CHINA

LEONARD EVERETT FISHER

Macmillan Publishing Company
New York

The red blocks seen throughout this book are called "chops." Since ancient times, Chinese artists have stamped their chops—their names or signs—on their work. Like a signature, a chop indicates who created the art. The chops in this book are Leonard Everett Fisher's initials in English and the sound of his name, "Len," in Chinese.

中原大國

Macmillan Publishing Company
866 Third Avenue, New York, NY 10022
Collier Macmillan Canada, Inc.

Printed in the United States of America

10 9 8 7 6 5 4 3 2

Library of Congress Cataloging-in-Publication Data
Fisher, Leonard Everett.
The Great Wall of China.
Summary: A brief history of the Great Wall of China, begun about 2,200 years ago to keep out Mongol invaders.
1. Great Wall of China (China) – History – Juvenile literature. [1. Great Wall of China (China) – History. 2. China – History – To 221 B.C.] I. Title.
DS793.G67F57   1986   931′.04   85-15324
ISBN 0-02-735220-X

C   H

With much appreciation to Kai Kwong Yung for his interest and scholarship in translating the illustration titles into Chinese

Chinese calligraphy by Shiu Wong Quan

The text of this book is set in ITC Zapf International Light. The illustrations are rendered in acrylic paints.

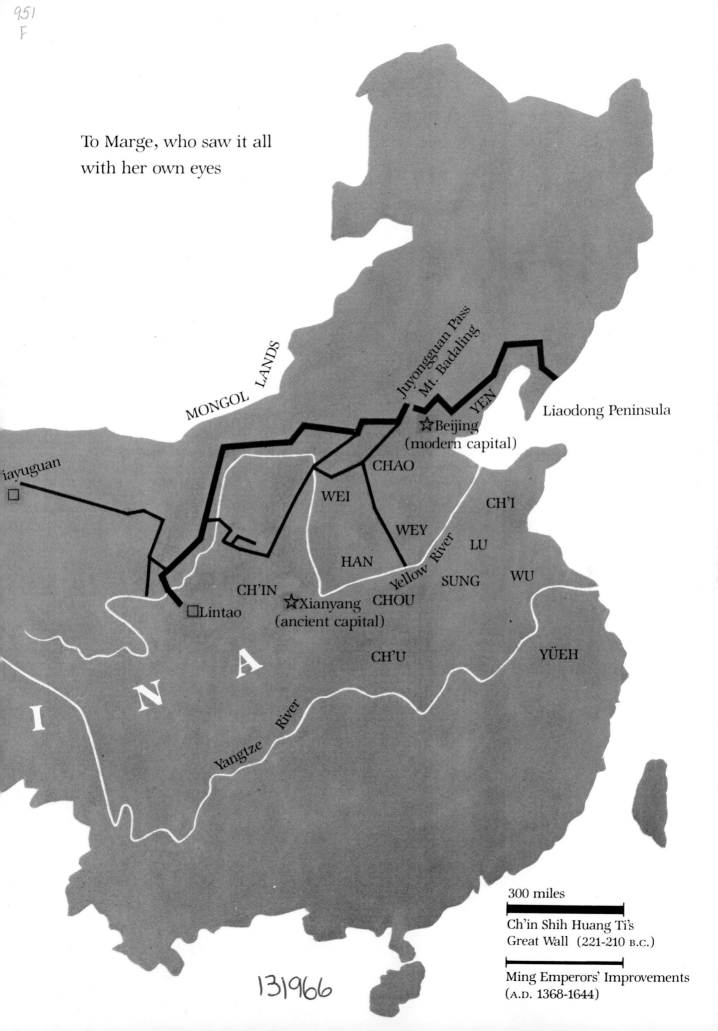

951
F

To Marge, who saw it all
with her own eyes

MONGOL LANDS

Juyongguan Pass
Mt. Badaling

YEN

Liaodong Peninsula

☆Beijing
(modern capital)

CHAO

WEI

CH'I

WEY

LU

HAN

Yellow River

SUNG

WU

iayuguan

CH'IN

CHOU

☐Lintao

☆Xianyang
(ancient capital)

I N A

CH'U

YÜEH

Yangtze River

131966

300 miles

Ch'in Shih Huang Ti's
Great Wall (221-210 B.C.)

Ming Emperors' Improvements
(A.D. 1368-1644)

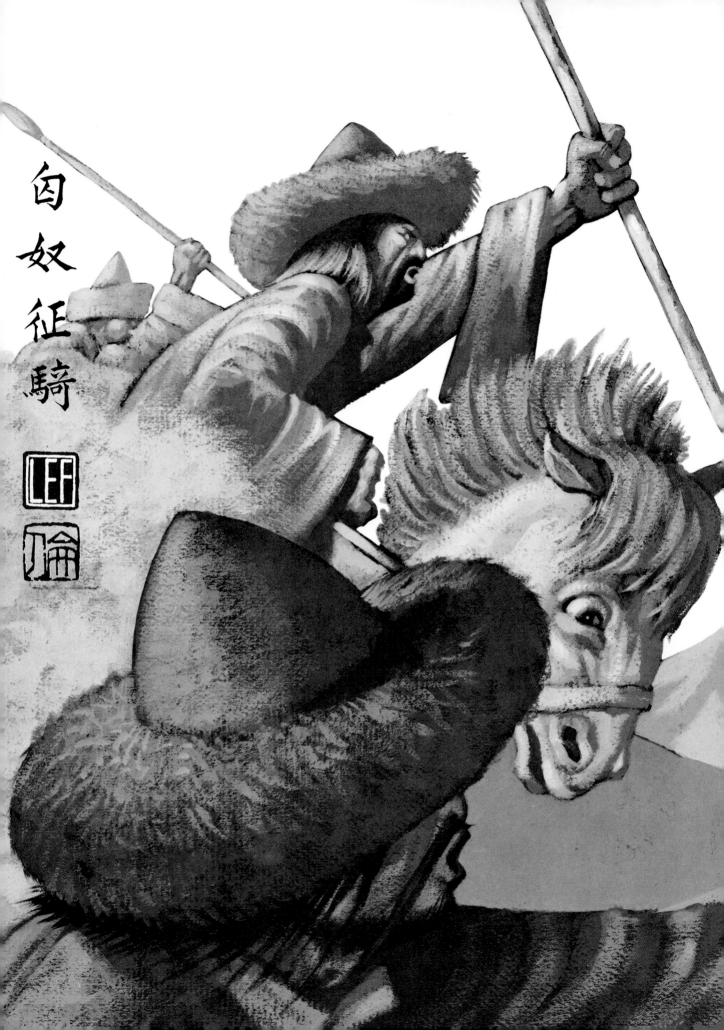

About twenty-two hundred years ago, King Cheng of Ch'in conquered the kingdoms of Han, Sung, Yen, Yüeh, Ch'i, Chou, Chao, Ch'u, Wei, Wey, Wu, and Lu. Tiny Ch'in became a huge empire: China. And King Cheng became Ch'in Shih Huang Ti, the First Supreme Emperor of China.

China was difficult to manage. Each of the old kingdoms had its own system of weights, measures, money, and writing. A grain of rice in Chao did not weigh the same in Chou. A hat size in Han was not the same in Sung. Money earned in Ch'i could not be spent in Ch'u. And officials in Wu could not read reports from officials in Lu. But the emperor brought order to his unwieldy lands. He made the systems of weights, measures, money, and writing the same everywhere. He even made everyone wear the same color: black.

Bringing order to his empire was not Ch'in Shih Huang Ti's only problem. In the north, fierce Mongol horsemen raided Chinese villages. They attacked the people and stole their goods. The Mongols threatened to invade all of China.

The guards flung a man at the emperor's feet. His clothes were torn and caked with mud. He had run a long way with his news. He trembled with fear.

"O Mighty Sire," he cried, "the Mongols have destroyed many villages in Wei. My own village has been turned to ashes. I alone have escaped."

Ch'in Shih Huang Ti rose in anger. "I must stop these barbarians!" he roared at the royal advisors.

8

龍顏震怒

"They are cruel," warned Li Ssu, the Prime Minister.

"They are tricky," added Chao Kao, Minister of the Household.

"And they are strong," declared Grand General Meng Tian.

"Soon they will fall on us," wailed the emperor's oldest son and Keeper of the Seals. "What will become of us? How shall we save ourselves?"

太師太保

蠻番夷狄

"With a wall!" Ch'in Shih Huang Ti bellowed.

"A wall? What wall?" the royal advisors asked. "We have many walls. None of them can stop these barbarians."

計上心頭

"I shall fix the old walls," replied the emperor. "I shall build a new and mightier wall and shall join all the walls together. I shall have one long wall across the top of China. It will stretch from Liaodong in the east to Lintao in the west. It will be six horses wide at the top, eight at the bottom, and five men high. I shall build it at the edge of our steepest mountains. No Mongol barbarian will be able to go around it, over it, under it, or through it. It will be the Great Wall!"

Ch'in Shih Huang Ti ordered Grand General Meng Tian to make preparations. The general's soldiers grabbed criminals, cheats, troublemakers, and anyone the emperor did not like. They dragged humble people from their homes. They forced musicians, teachers, writers, and artists to join the army of workers.

16 "And take that whining son of mine, Fu Su," the emperor commanded.

When all was ready, Grand General Meng Tian mounted his horse. With a wave of his arm, seven hundred thousand workers and three hundred thousand soldiers—one million people—marched north to build Ch'in Shih Huang Ti's Great Wall.

百萬雄師
匯輸

勞苦大衆

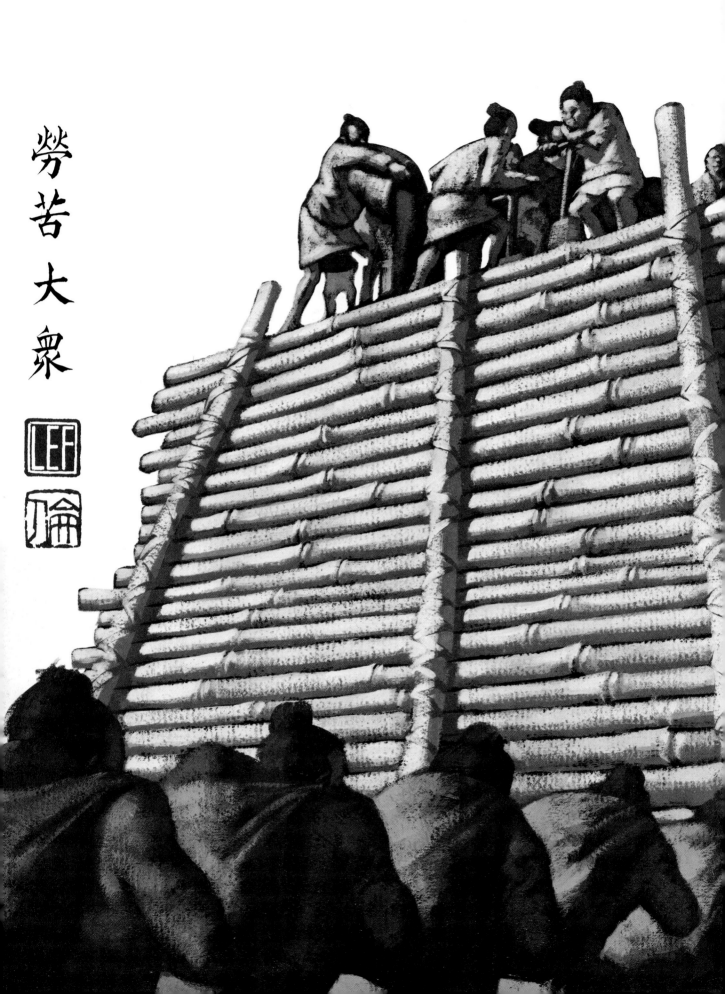

Tens of thousands were put to work fixing the old walls. Thousands more were made to pound the earth into thick, high mounds and to shape the mounds with bamboo poles.

砖墙石基

Mobs of workers made huge, heavy bricks from clay. They cut large, square stones as well. These they fitted to the sides and tops of the earthen mounds. The entire wall, from one end of Ch'in Shih Huang Ti's China to the other, they faced with brick and stone. 23

Every one hundred yards, the workers built watchtowers two stories high. Now the Mongols could be seen coming. Warning signals could be sent. There would be no more surprise attacks.

The Mongols watched from distant hills. They were unable to attack so many workers and soldiers on the high slopes.

烽火瞭臺

No one was allowed to rest.

"You, there!" screamed the soldiers, cracking their whips. "Faster! Faster! Work! Work! No idlers here!"

The Chinese worked day and night. Workers who complained or who ran away were caught and buried alive. Many workers lived out their lives building the wall. Many were buried in the wall.

婉轉延綿

The wall grew slowly, winding up and down the mountains. Roadways at the top were paved with three layers of brick. They connected the watchtowers. They were wide enough to hold ten soldiers side by side.

Finally, after ten years of labor, the wall was finished. Ch'in Shih Huang Ti came to inspect his Great Wall. He was overjoyed.

"I have stopped the Mongols," he shouted. "We are saved at last. Forever."

龍顏大悅

More about the Great Wall

Ch'in Shih Huang Ti was right. The Great Wall was so strong that the Mongols did not threaten China again for more than a thousand years. Later other emperors improved Ch'in Shih Huang Ti's Great Wall. The last improvements were made by the Ming emperors between A.D. 1368 and 1644. Today the Great Wall creeps across the north of China like a wounded dragon. Sections of the 3750 miles of wall lie in ruin. However, the People's Republic of China is restoring parts of the Great Wall. The wall will remain a testament to China's long history, her strength, and the constant toil of her people.

Translation of the Chinese Characters

2-3	The Great Wall
4-5	China
6-7	Mongol Horsemen
8-9	Angry Emperor
10-11	Royal Advisors
12-13	Barbarians
14-15	An Idea
16-17	Preparations
18-19	One Million Marchers
20-21	Laboring Thousands
22-23	Bricks and Stones
24-25	Watchtowers
26-27	Soldiers
28-29	Winding Wall
30-31	Happy Emperor